FOR HUNGRY DOGS EVERYWHERE,
hoping they get a tasty treat.

BOW WOW CHOW

HEARTY RECIPES
for HAPPY DOGS

Julia Szabo

CONTENTS

· · · · · · · · · · · ·

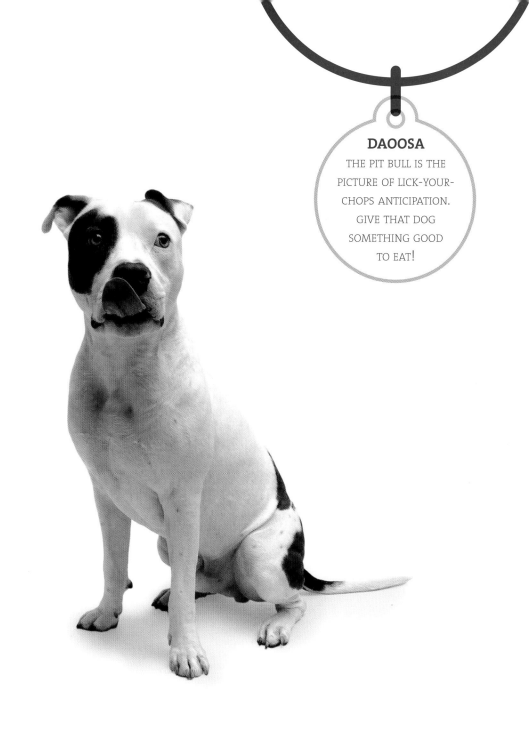

DAOOSA

THE PIT BULL IS THE
PICTURE OF LICK-YOUR-
CHOPS ANTICIPATION.
GIVE THAT DOG
SOMETHING GOOD
TO EAT!

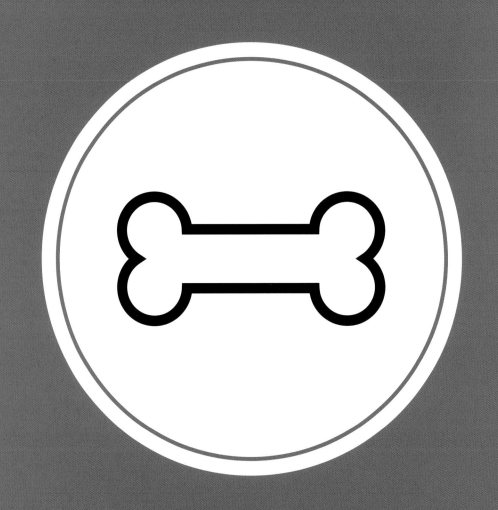

INTrODUCTION

To a dog, food is more than nourishment. It's a tangible, edible expression of love. The way Fido sees it, not to share food violates a basic tenet of the human-canine contract. Don't believe me? Then check out the intensely earnest expression on your dog's face the next time you dine in. To deny him table scraps, he seems to be saying, clearly means you don't care.

Some dogs know how to up their cuteness quotient to ensure that table scraps come their way. My Sam, for instance, makes an adorable noise that's part grunt and part oink; we call it "piggling." At dinner time, he sits by my leg and—ever so subtly—pumps up the piggle volume to guilt me into submission. If I'm slow on the uptake, he gently paws my leg. And, unless I'm partaking of something no dog should ever eat—anything containing onions, grapes, raisins, chocolate, or extremely spicy, salty, or sweet foods—resistance is futile. Sam scores every time (in moderation, of course).

You may be a gourmet, but your four-legged best friend has simpler tastes. An opportunistic omnivore, he's happy to gobble up anything that crosses his path, whether it's homemade delicacies or yesterday's garbage that someone neglected to throw out. We all know the difference between a gourmet and a gourmand; a gourmet is discerning, but a gourmand will stuff his face with just about anything. Your dog is a gourmand, all right—but not just any species of gourmand. He's a grrr-mand!

Yet, when Fido eats wholesome, quality food selected and prepared with care and the finest ingredients, we see the difference in his shiny coat, bright eyes, and happy attitude. That's incentive enough to make an effort, however small, toward upgrading his diet.

We think of cooking for dogs as something to do on very special occasions: their birthday, or when they feel unwell, or when

they travel with us to a swanky hotel that welcomes dogs. But before dog food was mass-produced, people cooked for their dogs as a matter of course. Dogs are not exactly strangers to the kitchen or pantry. The ancestor of all canines, the

If your takeout order contains no onions, it's fine to share a bite with Fido.

noble wolf, adapted himself from wild thing to house pet because it made more sense to partner with humans in the quest for food and safe shelter. To this day, "wolfing" is slang for devouring one's food like a wild animal. Fittingly, the wolf is the logical mascot for the Wolf Appliance Company of California, which recently merged with Sub-Zero to form an appliance powerhouse. Today, our busy schedules make catering daily dog-meals inconvenient—especially if, like me, you have more than one dog. Besides, prepared dog foods contain certain vitamins and minerals that dogs require for wellness.

As this book will prove, you needn't toss out your dog's favorite kibble to become a full-time chef. There are simple ways to enhance the flavor of your dog's food, enabling him to share in your feasts without harming him or inconveniencing

A heart-shaped dish and fancy ceramic bowl are two ways to tell a dog "I love you."

yourself—all while feeding yourself! Whether you have the energy to cook from scratch, prepare table scraps as dog-food 'garnish,' or just arrange ingredients in a dog bowl or plate, this book will give you a menu idea—or three—to whet human and canine appetites.

More than a strict recipe book, *Bow Wow Chow* is a lifestyle guide to enhancing everyday meals, with tips on what to eat, plus suggestions for tableware that will heighten the dining experience for humans and canines alike. Sharing is what it's all about!

There are some dogs (and people) who cannot eat certain foods or they risk serious illness. Dogs who suffer from allergies and are prescribed specific diets by their veterinarians must stick with that diet without deviation, or they risk an allergic reaction that, at its worst, could result in death. (Fortunately for these animals, Purina makes an excellent hypoallergenic diet called HA.) But for the rest, there is this book. Let the recipes and recommendations on these pages help you share every meal with your dog.

Enjoy. Or, as we say in our animal house, Bone Appétit!

Breakfast

———— 🦴 ————

Kibble à la Holstein

. . . .

Soft-boiled Eggs

. . . .

Breakfast Burrito

. . . .

Oatmeal

. . . .

Apple Pancakes

KIBBLE à la HOLSTEIN

Everyone loves eggs. Rich in protein and Biotin (a B vitamin) and one of the few foods that naturally contain vitamin D, eggs are a wonderful way to supplement a dog's meal, especially in the cold of winter, when everyone likes to feel warm and fortified. According to the Egg Nutrition Center, at the time of the French Revolution, Gallic gastronomes already knew 685 different ways of preparing eggs—including, of course, the omelet.

To avoid adding extra fat to your dog's diet, don't fry eggs—serve them soft-boiled instead for a healthier take on traditional Holstein. Your dog will enjoy the way the yolk and white combine to form a rich, kibble-enhancing gravy. In fact, your dog will enjoy just about everything about eggs, including the shells, which happen to be a fine source of calcium. (Just don't overdo it: Yolks also have cholesterol, so limit egg intake to one per dog, no more than twice a week, as elevated blood cholesterol increases the risk of heart disease in humans and dogs.) When you're done with your soft-boiled egg—served in an egg cup instead of a dog bowl—why not toss the extra shell to the dog too?

SOFT-BOILED EGGS

———————— 🦴 ————————

In a small covered pot, place eggs in water over high heat. When water begins to boil, time the eggs for exactly 2 minutes and 15 seconds. Cool the eggs by holding under cold running water. Break and serve over kibble.

For small dogs, break the shell into smaller pieces so it's easier for little teeth to chew.

RECOMMENDED SERVING: ONE EGG PER DOG

For small dogs, use a mortar and pestle to break the eggshell into bite-size bits before serving.

Breakfast Burrito

—━◆━—

Here's another way for humans and canines to share eggs—and a great way for busy, on-the-go types of both species to partake of breakfast even if they haven't got time to sit and eat.

2 white (or blue) corn tortillas   2 eggs, beaten
Olive oil

Preheat oven to 350°F. Heat tortillas in oven or in a toaster oven until warm but still soft. (Do not dry them out.) Using a wire whisk, beat eggs until frothy. Use an oil mister to spray a small amount of oil into a cast-iron pan. Heat over medium flame. Pour in eggs; allow to set about 1 minute, then swirl edges toward center. Allow to set again for about 1 minute. Turn off heat. Fold half of scrambled eggs into each tortilla and serve.

NOTE: Humans may add excitement to their breakfast burrito by adding shredded Cheddar cheese and/or hot sauce.

MAKES ONE BURRITO FOR A LARGE DOG (ONE SERVES TWO SMALL DOGS) AND ONE FOR A HUMAN

a.m. oatmeal

You don't have to be Scottish to appreciate oats—they're a wonderful way for humans and canines to start the day together. Of course, Sheba the border collie mix is Scottish—Border collies originated in the border country between Scotland and England. Wherever you happen to be, oatmeal is a heart-healthy breakfast for you and your dog, and the simplest way for you both to share food. While you probably take yours with a splash of cream or maple sugar (I like mine with blueberry preserves), your dog enjoys his plain or sprinkled with kibble—hold everything else.

My dogs and I agree: steel-cut oats have the most pleasing

For humans and canines, a bowl of oats is a heart-healthy way to start the day.

texture, especially when they've been soaked in water overnight for maximum tenderness the next morning. When sharing with dogs, just be sure to prepare oats with water, not milk, as the canine digestive system doesn't tolerate dairy products. "Dogs are like lactose-intolerant people," explains Dr. Heather Peikes, allergy specialist and founder of Animal Allergy and Dermatology Specialists in New York City. "They lack the enzyme to break down milk, and can get diarrhea if they ingest milk in large amounts."

SHEBA
IS PROUD OF HER
SCOTCH HERITAGE; NOTE
THE JAUNTY
TAM-O-SHANTER
ON HER PRETTY
HEAD.

apple of my eye

My dogs are nuts for apples, whether sliced and served raw (they happily devour them, especially Cortlands and Macintoshes, seeded and cored) or baked into a moist, delicious apple cake. Watching

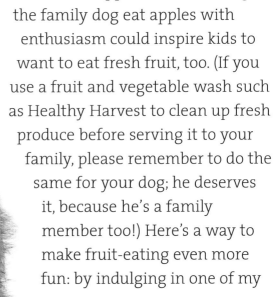

the family dog eat apples with enthusiasm could inspire kids to want to eat fresh fruit, too. (If you use a fruit and vegetable wash such as Healthy Harvest to clean up fresh produce before serving it to your family, please remember to do the same for your dog; he deserves it, because he's a family member too!) Here's a way to make fruit-eating even more fun: by indulging in one of my

favorite breakfast options—apple pancakes. This is a downright decadent treat, and it's not for every day. But on a cold winter morning, it's a heavenly breakfast delight that will fill the kitchen with the most inviting aroma imaginable.

Healthy Harvest vegetable wash gets fresh produce clean and green.

TIP

Take it from Ellie the mini-mutt (opposite)—on special mornings indulge in decadent apple pancakes.

apple pancakes

2 apples, peeled, cored, and very thinly sliced
Cinnamon and nutmeg to taste

All-natural pancake mix, such as Arrowhead Mills
2 tablespoons clarified butter*

Sprinkle the apple slices with the cinnamon and nutmeg. In a medium bowl, mix pancake batter according to package directions; then add clarified butter. Warm a non-stick frying pan over medium heat. Pour about ¼ cup of pancake batter into pan (less if you want a smaller pancake). Carefully lay out a few apple slices on top of pancake. When craters and bubbles form on the top of the pancake, it's time to flip it. Cook a few more minutes, until golden brown. Serve a stack of pancakes to humans with maple syrup; serve one pancake, plain, to your dog.

*NOTE: To clarify butter: Heat in a saucepan over low heat until it crackles and bubbles. Remove the pan from the heat and skim the milk solids off the melted butter.

SERVES TWO PEOPLE AND ONE OR TWO DOGS

LUNCH

—— ▪━▪ ——

Coco's Meatballs

· · · · · · · · ·

Pasta alla Giulia

· · · · · · · · ·

Fiona's Fish Cakes

· · · · · · · · ·

Stewed Chicken Wraps

· · · · · · · · ·

Chef John Iachetti's Chow Hound Beef

COCO

KEEPS HER GIRLISH
FIGURE BY LIMITING
HERSELF TO JUST ONE
HIGH-CARB TREAT
PER WEEK.

LUNCHEON WITH COCO

Coco the Caniche (that's French for Poodle) adores whole-wheat bagels. But you know what they say about the French, especially the females of the species: They know instinctively how to avoid getting fat. With remarkable discipline, Coco keeps her girlish figure by limiting herself to just one high-carb treat per week. Here, she's already allowed herself her bagel ration, so she's able to sit calmly while faced with temptation. (Most dogs, on the other hand—mine included—don't possess Coco's Gallic self-restraint, and would devour the lot in a flash. That's why I have to keep all food in my kitchen safely out of the dogs' reach!)

Like many dogs, Coco eats a daily mixture of kibble and canned dog food. Sprinkled over her bowl, however, is a very special "garnish": one homemade turkey meatball, crumbled into bite-size pieces. These meatballs keep in the refrigerator for a few days; they make a wonderful hors d'oeuvre for a (human) cocktail party (especially with some honey mustard dipping sauce), a garnish for a simple plate of pasta, or a fun lunch or dinner guaranteed to bring a smile to a finicky child's lips.

coco's meatballs

1 pound lean ground turkey
1 cup bread crumbs
½ cup chopped mushrooms
½ cup coarsely chopped
  parsley

2 egg whites
Dash of grated Parmesan cheese
3 drops Worcestershire or
  Teriyaki sauce

In a medium bowl, combine all ingredients thoroughly and form into small meatballs.

Grill the meatballs on an indoor grill for about 5 minutes on each side until golden brown (they will be flatter as a result, resembling miniature burgers), or bake in the oven at 350°F for 25 minutes until golden brown (retaining the meatballs' nice, round shape).

YIELD: 24 MEATBALLS

NOTE: To modify the recipe for humans-only consumption: Substitute finely chopped scallions for parsley; mix in a few more dashes of Parmesan cheese; and add an Italian seasoning mixture containing oregano, basil, and other spices, plus sea salt and freshly ground pepper to taste.

OPTIONAL: Roll meatballs in sesame seeds prior to baking, for an even tastier crust.

STAYING HYDRATED

If you're a health-conscious person, chances are you filter your tap water before drinking it or serving it to guests. And yet, many people don't think to filter the water they set down for their dogs. Perhaps the single most important thing you can share with your best friend—and the simplest to prepare!— is fresh, filtered water. (If you haven't got a filter or you're on the road, use bottled water.) Besides ridding water of unwanted chemicals and sediments, the Brita filtration system is convenient and easy on the eyes—especially if it's the collectible pitcher designed by architect Michael Graves. And if you moisten your dog's kibble with water, please use the filtered or bottled water for that too.

Make water available to your dog at all times, in a ceramic or metal bowl that's washed often.

NACO

THE SHIBA INU
INSISTS ON DRINKING
FILTERED WATER—AND
WE BET YOUR DOG
DOES TOO.

TIP

Don't go overboard with carbs such as bread, potatoes, rice, or any kind of noodle or pasta. Your dog can have a few strands of linguine, but certainly not the entire bowl. That would be too much of a good thing.

Mangia!

Luca, a Spinone Italiano (Italian pointer) proves by his affinity for pasta that he's Italian through and through—as Italian, in fact, as the tricolor flag of his native land, or the *tricolore* of basil and tomato in a white Fiesta dog bowl. (When he's not ciao-ing down, Luca also howls along to Italian opera!) When sharing pasta sauce with dogs, a simple *pomodoro e olio* is best, for it brings hearty flavor to a dog's regular food without endangering him with onions, which are harmful to him. Spoon the plain tomato-oil sauce over Fido's kibble and include a few strands of pasta and a basil sprig as a garnish. (This simple sauce is also an enticing way to encourage finicky kids to graduate from plain noodles to pasta with sauce.)

If, like me, you cook with onions and red wine in your sauce, you'll need to prepare the sauce in two stages, using two separate pans. The goal is to avoid "contaminating" the tomato sauce with ingredients that don't agree with Fido, namely, onions and wine. As you'll see, it's simple to prepare these tasty extras separately, then fold them in to the portion you spoon over your dish of pasta.

pasta alla giulia

6 tablespoons extra-virgin olive oil

One 28-ounce can crushed tomatoes

1 package spinach pasta

1 large onion, coarsely chopped

6 cloves garlic, crushed

Salt and freshly ground black or white pepper to taste

1 ½ cups good red wine, such as Montepulciano or Cabernet

Grated Pecorino Romano or Parmigiano Reggiano

2 leafy sprigs fresh basil

Heat 4 tablespoons of olive oil in a stainless-steel pan over medium-high heat. Add crushed tomatoes to the center of the pan in 4-tablespoon increments. Stir quickly until puree combines with oil to form a glaze; take care not to burn the tomato sauce. Add more puree and repeat; keep adding until puree can is empty. Lower heat, transfer to a back burner, and simmer while preparing pasta water to boil.

Cook pasta in boiling water, until *al dente*.

In a separate pan, heat 2 tablespoons olive oil over medium-high heat. Sauté onions and garlic, seasoned with salt and pepper, until soft and brown around the edges. Pour in wine, cover, and lower heat.

Keeping the tomato sauce and the "extras" separate, serve Fido his kibble with a few spoonfuls of tomato sauce, a few strands of pasta, and a fresh basil garnish. Combine your tomato sauce with the onion-garlic-wine mixture, pour over pasta, and season with grated Romano or Parmigiano Reggiano. Garnish with basil.

NOTE: Simplest way to soup up a bowl of dog food, all'Italiana: Use an oil mister to lend the rich flavor of extra-virgin olive oil to plain, dry kibble. This is safe to do every day. In winter, when human and canine skin dries out from the cold, try adding flaxseed oil once weekly to your dog's food, and watch his coat become glossier and his skin noticeably less dry.

SERVES FOUR PEOPLE AND ONE DOG, OR TWO PEOPLE AND ONE DOG, WITH ENOUGH LEFT OVER FOR ONE MORE LUNCH OR DINNER

FIONA'S FISH CAKES

More and more dog-food companies are recognizing that dogs like the taste of fish almost as much as cats. Here's a recipe that's easy to make, and even easier to share. Incidentally, parsley is a natural breath freshener, which is important when indulging in seafood treats!

1 pound fresh boneless salmon fillet
2 tablespoons olive oil
1 large egg, lightly beaten
2 tablespoons mayonnaise

2 tablespoons Dijon mustard
6 tablespoons breadcrumbs
3 tablespoons finely chopped fresh parsley
Salt and freshly ground pepper

Preheat the oven to 400°F. Place salmon in a baking dish; rub with 1 tablespoon oil. Roast fish in oven until cooked through, about 15 minutes. Let cool completely, then pat dry with paper towels. Rake fish with a fork.

In a large bowl, combine salmon, egg, mayonnaise, mustard, breadcrumbs, and parsley. Mix very gently, until ingredients bind together. Form mixture into small patties.

Heat 1 tablespoon oil in a nonstick pan over medium heat. Cook cakes until golden brown, about 2 minutes on each side.

NOTE: To modify for humans, add salt and freshly ground pepper to the batter. Serve Fido's portion plain; serve humans' portion with tartar sauce.

SERVES FOUR PEOPLE AND TWO DOGS

STeWeD CHICKeN WraPS

———————— 🦴 ————————

3 large spinach or tomato
   flour tortillas
Stewed chicken meat, reserved
   from Chicken Soup
   (see recipe, page 57)

Dijon mustard and horseradish
   to taste

Preheat oven to 350°F. Heat tortillas in oven until warm but still soft. (Do not dry them out.) Carefully separate meat from bones. Arrange meat on one quarter of a flat tortilla; fold and wrap until tortilla holds meat securely. Enjoy!

NOTE: To modify for humans, add mustard and horseradish. Leave canine portion plain.

SERVES TWO PEOPLE AND TWO LARGE DOGS

CHEF JOHN IACHETTI'S CHOW HOUND BEEF

---●───

Regency Hotel, NYC

This is a popular item on the room-service menu for canine guests at the swank Regency Hotel on New York City's Park Avenue. Now traveling dogs can enjoy this delicacy at home (and if the recipe is doubled, humans can share in the fun).

6 ounces diced beef
Olive oil
4 ounces white rice

2 ounces haricots verts
2 ounces diced carrots
2 ounces diced broccoli

In a skillet, sauté the beef in olive oil over medium-high heat . Cook for about 10 to 15 minutes.

Steam the rice and vegetables separately. Once meat is cooked, combine with rice and steamed vegetables, and serve in a dog bowl.

SERVES ONE DOG

DINNER

—— ᚙ ——

Steak au Poivre/Steak au Naturel

· · · · · · · · ·

Grrreat Grrrilled Vegetables

· · · · · · · · ·

Lamb Shanks D'Artagnan

· · · · · · · · ·

Chicken Paprikash

· · · · · · · · ·

Chicken Soup

· · · · · · · · ·

*Chef John Villa's
Braised Veal Osso Buco*

· · · · · · · · ·

Just Gravy

PEPPER

THE PIT BULL IS SUCH
A FOODIE THAT SHE IS
EVEN NAMED AFTER
A SEASONING; HER
NICKNAME IS POIVRE
(FRENCH FOR PEPPER).

TODAY'S
SPECIAL

~~FRIED CHICKEN~~

~~ONION SOUP~~

STEAK !

steak au poivre/ steak au naturel

Human gourmets can't resist a steak au poivre that's fragrant with a generous sprinkling of freshly ground black and white pepper, plus other spices, to create a flavorful crust. But for canine grrrmands, whose digestions don't always agree with spices, it's safer to serve steak au naturel.

The solution: Share a high-protein dinner with your best friend by preparing two separate steaks on an indoor grill. One sirloin is moistened with a light misting of olive oil; the other is oiled, then covered with pepper, coarse grains of sea salt, and a dusting of wonderfully aromatic nutmeg.

An oil mister is a tool that comes in handy when cooking with canines.

Steak au Poivre/ Steak au Naturel

Pre-heat an indoor grill according to the manufacturer's directions. For the Steak au Naturel, lightly moisten your choice of beef cut with olive oil using a mister. For the Steak au Poivre, mist with olive oil, then season liberally to taste with freshly ground black, white, and/or pink peppercorns, coarse sea salt, and freshly grated nutmeg. Place on opposite sides of the grill, and cook until desired doneness is reached.

NOTE: While you may be tempted to devour your entire steak, please don't feed Fido's to him all at once; it's too much of a good thing. Give your dog a smaller portion and refrigerate the rest. Remember, steak is just as delicious—if not more so—served cold, as a kibble-enhancer.

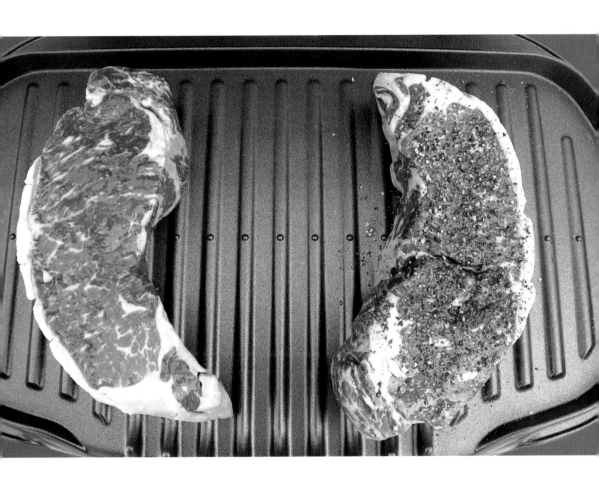

To keep things safely separate, we use the Foreman Double Knockout grill

Grrreat Grrrilled Vegetables

While you've got the grill fired up, might as well grill some vegetables as a side dish. Dogs and humans agree that zucchini and yellow squash grill up especially well—and make a fine side dish to complement grilled meat.

2 medium sized zucchinis   Olive oil
2 medium sized yellow squash

Wash vegetables with a natural vegetable wash, such as Healthy Harvest, and running water. Cut vegetables lengthwise into ¼-inch slices, spray with oil from an oil mister, and grill for a few minutes until tender.

NOTE: Dogs take their grilled veggies unseasoned, but humans can dress up their portion with salt, pepper, balsamic vinegar . . . whatever appeals. If baby zucchini and squash are in season, simply use double the amount and cut them in half.

Lamb Shanks D'Artagnan

D'Artagnan the Welsh terrier has a list of favorite snack foods, including mango, goat cheese, almonds, and Brazil nuts—but when he is serious about tucking into a hearty dinner-time meal, he requests this lamb dish.

6 lamb shanks, about
  1 pound each
Olive oil
1 cup white rice

1 cup carrots, peeled and
  coarsely chopped
1 cup frozen peas
1 clove garlic, crushed
3 cups water

Mist a large, deep skillet with oil and heat. Add lamb shanks and brown on all sides over medium-high heat. Remove from pan and set aside. Meanwhile cook the rice according to package directions. Add the carrots, peas, and garlic to the skillet and cook over medium heat, stirring occasionally until soft. Add water to the skillet and bring to a boil. Turn the heat to low. Return the lamb shanks to the skillet and cook for about 30 minutes, turning the shanks a few times. Simmer until meat is tender. Serve with rice.

NOTE: To modify for humans, add salt and freshly ground pepper.

SERVES FOUR PEOPLE AND TWO DOGS

KIPLING

THE CHAMPION
VIZSLA LOOKS QUITE
READY TO DEVOUR A
HELPING OF CHICKEN
PAPRIKASH.

Kiss Me,
I'm Hungarian

No one could be more Hungarian than the handsome hound known as the Vizsla. His intelligent expression gave rise to the Magyar saying "olyan mint egy Vizsla" ("alert as a Vizsla")—and he always looks extra-alert whenever his people are busy cooking classic Magyar dishes such as Chicken Paprikash. Traditionally, this delicious recipe calls for two onions, but onions are not good for dogs. Besides, the lovely flavor and cheerful color of the red peppers more than compensate for the onions' absence—in fact, they pump up the "paprika" quotient ("paprika," after all, is Hungarian for pepper).

When sharing Hungarian delicacies with dogs, use sweet paprika instead of hot.

CHICKEN PAPRIKASH

3 strips bacon
1 large red pepper, seeded
  and finely chopped
1 whole chicken, cut into
  pieces, or 4 chicken legs
1 teaspoon salt
1 tablespoon sweet
  Hungarian paprika

1 medium-sized ripe tomato,
  chopped
1 green pepper, seeded and
  finely chopped
2 teaspoons all-purpose flour
½ cup yogurt

Cook bacon in a saucepan; when done, remove meat and leave fat. Add red peppers and sauté until softened. Add chicken, salt, and paprika and stir.

Brown chicken on all sides, about 5 minutes. Cover and simmer slowly, adding water now and then as necessary. After ½ hour, add tomato and green pepper. When meat is tender, about an hour later, sprinkle with flour and stir in yogurt. Cook, uncovered,

10 minutes longer. Serve with pasta or homemade dumplings.

NOTE: To modify the recipe for humans who like it hot: Replace yogurt with sour cream and substitute 1 hot pepper (such as jalapeño) for the green pepper and hot paprika for sweet.

SERVES TWO PEOPLE AND TWO DOGS, WITH ENOUGH LEFT OVER FOR ONE LUNCH PLUS ONE DOG SNACK

When sharing food with pets, presentation can still be fun. This traditional hand-painted Hungarian platter is a fine example.

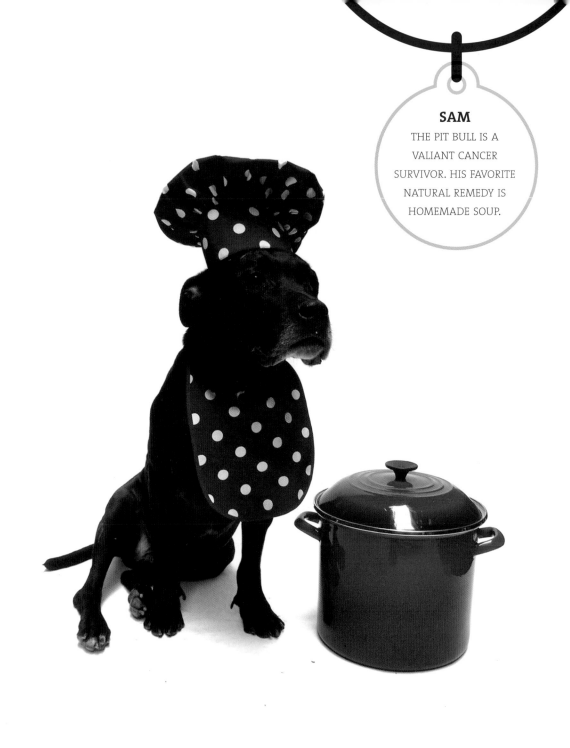

SAM

THE PIT BULL IS A VALIANT CANCER SURVIVOR. HIS FAVORITE NATURAL REMEDY IS HOMEMADE SOUP.

sam's chicken soup

Nothing warms the spirit better than chicken soup, for molten chicken fat has curative properties found in no other food. Little wonder every culture around the world has its chicken soup recipe. Take it from my dog, Chef Sam: This recipe results in a very mild broth, thanks largely to the omission of two chicken-soup staples, onions and spices. But that's just fine for delicate canine digestions. A cup or two of Sam's soup ladled over some kibble—or even some plain white rice—makes a fine meal. Just be sure to skim off all the excess pools of gleaming fat, as too much fat is not good for dogs. It can lead to a condition called pancreatitis, an inflammation of the pancreas caused by excessive additions of fat to the canine diet; for this reason, bacon, beef tallow, and poultry skins are to be avoided as well.

feeding dogs, starving cancer

My Sam has spent the last couple of years waging a brave battle against cancer. To help him fight this fierce, tireless opponent, we make every effort to give him a low-carb diet that's also free of sugar, as cancer cells thrive on anything starchy or sweet (salt is also a no-no). That means no carrots, sweet potatoes, or apples—and certainly no pasta or bread, although Sam could melt a heart of stone begging for both.

If your dog has cancer, eliminate the carrots from the foregoing soup recipe, and replace them with burdock; this versatile root is prized as a cancer preventative. And don't be overzealous about skimming off all those gleaming pools of chicken fat—cancer cells don't like fat. Your dog will be thrilled to slurp a fattier portion of soup, and with that extra-rich, extra-flavorful helping, he won't even notice the lack of carbs, sugar, or salt!

To spice things up for human consumption, simply keep sea salt and freshly ground pepper on hand, and serve with thin slices of daikon radish, plus some mustard and horseradish as condiments for the stewed meat. (Beware of sharing radishes with canines: They cause serious flatulence!)

Dogs like eating soup from a bowl with a rubber ring to prevent sliding.

SAM'S CHICKEN SOUP

1 whole chicken
5 stalks celery, untrimmed

5 carrots, untrimmed
Few sprigs parsley or dill

With a piece of string, tie the chicken in unbleached cheesecloth so that bones can't float all over the place. Place chicken, plus all other ingredients, in a large stockpot. Fill pot with filtered water to cover. Bring to a boil; lower heat, and simmer for 2 hours.

Remove chicken and debone; set meat aside. Reserve cartilage tips from bones as a nutritional treat: the cartilage contains glucosamine, which helps old, stiff canine joints to stay lubricated and working properly.

To make the soup ultra-kid-friendly, boil fun-shaped noodles or orzo, not in water, but in a few cups of chicken broth, for the number of minutes specified on the package. The noodles will be unbelievably rich and delicious. (This was my favorite menu item as a youngster, and it's still my ultimate comfort food.)

SERVES FOUR PEOPLE AND TWO DOGS, WITH PLENTY OF LEFTOVERS

CHEF JOHN VILLA'S BRAISED OSSO BUCCO

───── 🦴 ─────

Chef John Villa, whose New York City restaurants Dominic (see page 95) and Patroon are favorite destinations of gourmets on two and four legs, has a beloved Doberman named Rin Tin Tin, so he understands how to satisfy a big dog's powerful appetite.

4 veal shanks, 10 ounces each
Salt and freshly ground pepper
   to taste
6 tablespoons olive oil
1 cup diced carrot
1 cup diced parsnip
1 cup diced celery

2 cloves garlic
4 tablespoons tomato paste
¾ cup white wine*
1 bay leaf
1 bunch thyme
3 cups chicken or veal stock

Preheat oven to 350°F.

In a heavy skillet on high heat, season the shanks with salt and pepper, add the oil to the pan, and sear shanks until well-browned on all sides. Do not overcrowd the pan; if the pan is not big enough, do one at a time.

Place shanks in an oven-proof casserole and reserve. To the skillet add the vegetables and garlic and sauté 4 to 5 minutes, then add the tomato paste and cook for an additional 2 to 3 minutes. Deglaze with the white wine, reduce by half, and pour over the shanks. Add bay leaf and thyme. Heat the stock until boiling in a separate pot and pour over the shanks.

Cover and braise in oven for 1 ½ to 2 hours, or until the meat easily pulls away from the bone. Remove from the pan and reduce the cooking liquid until it has a light sauce consistency, then pour over the shanks and serve.

Remember, don't serve cooked bones to the dog—only the marrow!

*NOTE: The small amount of wine called for in this recipe won't hurt a dog, as its alcohol content will almost entirely evaporate in cooking.

SERVES TWO PEOPLE AND TWO LARGE DOGS, WITH LEFTOVERS

JUST Gravy

— 🦴 —

Who can resist a generous helping of gravy? This recipe is enhanced by the wonderful flavor and texture of healthful shiitake mushrooms, and thickened with katakuriko powder, made from the starch of the dog-tooth violet, which grows in Japan (katakuriko is far superior to flour or corn starch, for it thickens with no lumps). The resulting gravy makes a rich, smooth, irresistible addition to your dog's kibble— or your mashed potatoes.

2 ounces shiitake mushrooms, including stems; cut off the tough stem tips and slice the caps

1 cup beef stock (see recipe, page 73)

3 tablespoons katakuriko powder

Simmer mushrooms with stock; thicken by stirring in katakuriko.

NOTE: If using dried shiitake mushrooms, soak for 30 minutes in a bowl of warm water before starting recipe. Add soaking water to the simmering vegetable stock for extra flavor and add in 1 extra teaspoon of katakuriko to compensate for the extra liquid.

SERVES TWO PEOPLE AND ONE OR TWO DOGS

after Dinner Mints

To clear the palate after a meal, we humans have breath mints, toothbrushes, and toothpaste. To help keep their choppers clean and healthy and their breath fresh, dogs have dental bones. Gnawing on these helps keep a canine's canines healthy and strong. Not all green bones are created equal, however: be sure to insist on Breath-A-Licious, which trounces its empty-calorie competition with natural, breath-freshening ingredients such as fennel, dill, chlorophyll, peppermint oil, and parsley oil (peppermint is also a natural digestive aid to help keep Fido's stomach calm). The best part? Unlike real-meat bones, which leave a tell-tale trail on home furnishings, the Breath-A-Licious won't mess up your favorite upholstery fabric (especially if it's ultra-durable material by Crypton SuperFabric, in a canine pattern designed by artist William Wegman).

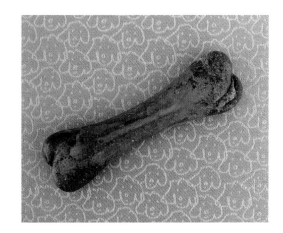

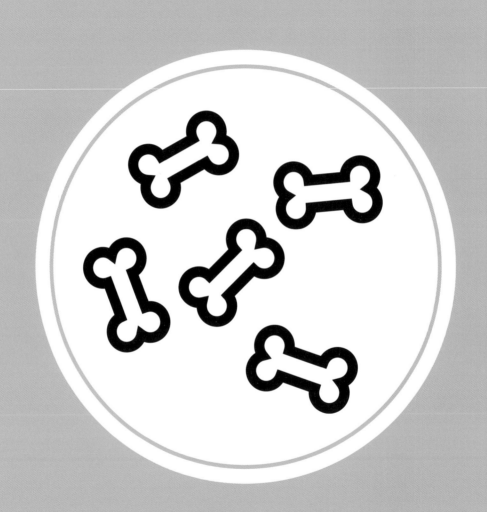

SNACKS

— ᚖ —

Carrots

· · · · · · · ·

Popcorn

· · · · · · · ·

Sue's Tasty Training Treats

· · · · · · · ·

Mmm Mmm Hummmus

· · · · · · · ·

Raw Bone

· · · · · · · ·

Basic Beef Stock

· · · · · · · ·

Really Rewarding Rewards

carrot tips

Dogs are opportunistic omnivores: although they adore meat, they also enjoy varying their diet with vegetables, fruit, and grains. Vegetables are as healthful for dogs as they are for people, and feeding the occasional veggie to the dog is one way to encourage a veggie-protesting child to eat what's good for him.

Carrots are a favorite with canines because they are crunchy and sweet. Some dogs—like Billie the mutt—will even do tricks in exchange for a carrot reward! If you know your dog loves carrots, keep a bag or two of pre-peeled baby carrots in your refrigerator and use them in training sessions as handy bite-sized incentives. When I find enormous carrots like the one in the photograph, I sometimes give them to my dogs as a chew-bone (this also works with burdock root, which happens to be a known

Use a decorative vegetable cutter to turn carrots into appealing shapes.

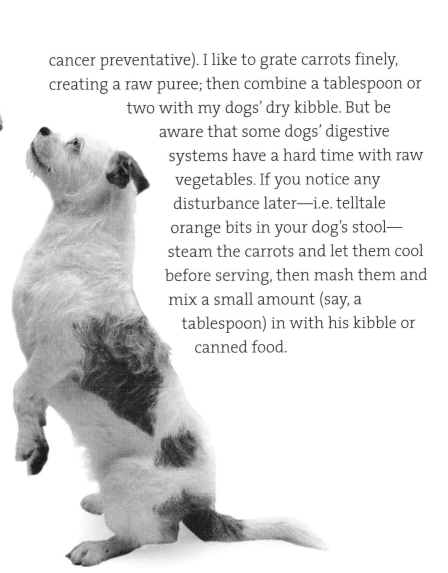

cancer preventative). I like to grate carrots finely, creating a raw puree; then combine a tablespoon or two with my dogs' dry kibble. But be aware that some dogs' digestive systems have a hard time with raw vegetables. If you notice any disturbance later—i.e. telltale orange bits in your dog's stool— steam the carrots and let them cool before serving, then mash them and mix a small amount (say, a tablespoon) in with his kibble or canned food.

BOOMER

THE MUTT
CONTEMPLATES A
CRISPY MORSEL OF
FRESH POPCORN.

aNYTIMe SNackK: POPCORN

I have yet to meet the person or dog who doesn't love fresh, hot popcorn— it's simply the most perfect, irresistible snack food there is. (My late beagle absolutely adored the stuff, and I couldn't resist treating him to it often.) But popcorn isn't much without a generous helping of seasoning, whether plain sea salt, grated cheddar or Parmesan cheese, or a spicy blend of curry and cayenne pepper. Since too many add-ons can upset your dog's stomach, prepare two separate bowls of the crispy white stuff. Season yours with whatever pleases you, and toss Fido's portion with a small amount of Dinner Party, a safe yet tasty seasoning created especially for canines; it comes in three flavors, Salmon, Beef, and Chicken. Be aware, however, that corn is a common allergen in dogs, so if your dog experiences diarrhea or hives, please don't feed him popcorn, or corn in any form.

sue's Tasty Training Treats

———— ✁ ————

My friend Sue Nastasi is a dog trainer in New York City who works with a wide variety of dogs, from pampered pets to hard-working therapy dogs. She always achieves excellent results with her trainees—and the secret is not just her expertise and gentle bedside manner. Like the best behaviorists working with dogs today, Sue believes in positive reinforcement, so she always makes sure to have tasty treats on hand, to motivate her charges to do what she asks of them. Her surefire motivator? Bite-size bits of baked chicken.

2 chicken breasts
Olive Oil

Preheat oven to 350°F. Spray chicken breasts lightly on both sides with oil from an oil mister. Place on a baking sheet and bake for 45 minutes on each side. Let cool, and cut into bite-size pieces.

NOTE: To make yourself a chicken sandwich or salad, season to taste with lemon juice, fresh garlic, salt, and pepper.

SERVES ONE LARGE DOG OR FOUR SMALL ONES

MMM MMM HUMMMUS

This delightful Mediterranean dip is always a crowd-pleaser so it's perfect party food, and a perfectly safe snack to share with a favorite dog. Serve it with wedges of warm pita bread, chunks of fresh red pepper, and—my dogs' and my favorite— seedless cucumber slices.

2 cups canned chick peas, drained and rinsed
3 cloves fresh garlic, pressed
3 tablespoons lemon juice
½ cup water

3 tablespoons tahini (sesame paste)
1 teaspoon paprika
Olive oil
1 lemon, cut into wedges
3 sprigs fresh parsley, minced

Combine chick peas in food processor with garlic, lemon juice, and water. Process until smooth, about 1 minute. Add more water if consistency is too thick. Stir in tahini and paprika, and add more lemon juice to taste. Transfer dip to a bowl; mist with oil, and serve with lemon wedges and chopped fresh parsley.

SERVES FOUR PEOPLE AND FOUR DOGS

DOG WITH BONE

It's universal shorthand for tenacity: the proverbial "dog with a bone." But to present your dog with a real, raw bone is to understand how that expression came into parlance! Attempts to improve on nature's ultimate chew toy haven't perfected the raw beef bone; dogs will gladly spend as long as necessary to extract every last morsel of marrow from the bone's cavity. And chewing on the bone itself is a fine workout for a dog's teeth, helping to keep them in great condition.

Fortunately, beef bones are quite inexpensive, whether purchased from your local butcher or ordered online from an organic meat-parts supplier. So if you hate leaving your dog alone, give him a raw beef bone prior to leaving to alleviate your guilt; Fido might not even notice you're gone. The only drawback? Raw bones leave behind a spectacular, gory mess. Be sure to slipcover your furniture with a durable, washable material such as Crypton SuperFabric, which comes clean with ease, or close the dog into the kitchen while he chews to his heart's content and give the floor a good swabbing after.

Please serve only raw bones; don't ever give cooked bones to any pet. During cooking, bones harden, becoming so brittle that they splinter easily. The injuries that could result, including

MILO

THE MUTT USES
BOTH FRONT PAWS TO
HOLD ON TIGHT TO
HIS BELOVED BEEF
BONE.

intestinal punctures, can be fatal. Better safe than sorry: always go with raw.

Dogs get uncooked bones, but humans stew bones for several hours with a variety of ingredients until they yield a hearty, delicious broth. This simple stock is the foundation for any number of delicious mid-winter soups and gravies that you and your dog can share. Hopefully, your freezer is big enough to hold enough bones for your dog's raw enjoyment as well as your cooking needs (if it's a Sub-Zero, it's definitely big enough). Just remember that chewing cooked bones is hazardous to dogs' health, so take care to eliminate temptation by discarding the cooked bones when you're done cooking, so Fido won't root through the trash in search of them.

TIP

Never, ever give your dog any kind of cooked bone, no matter how hard he begs for it. Cooked bones can splinter and cause serious intestinal punctures.

BASIC BEEF STOCK

8 pounds beef soup bones
12 cups water, plus ⅓ cup
   for rinsing pan

⅓ cup cubed potatoes
2 bay leaves

Preheat oven to 350°F. Place soup bones in a large roasting pan and bake, uncovered, about 25 minutes, turning the bones occasionally until browned.

Drain off fat and place the bones in a stockpot. Add ⅓ cup water to roasting pan and deglaze pan, pouring liquid into stockpot. Add potato cubes and bay leaves plus 12 cups of water.

Bring to a boil, then reduce heat. Cover and simmer for 4 to 5 hours. Strain stock through a sieve lined with a piece of unbleached cheesecloth.

SERVES FOUR PEOPLE AND FOUR DOGS

TAKING THE TOFU TEST

Whether made of soy (tofu) or wheat (seitan), meat substitutes such as Chickettes, Smart Dogs, or Tofu Pups have come a long way. When preparing vegetarian recipes, especially for children who refuse to eat meat, it's great fun to experiment with creative meat substitutes. If you're trying out a new brand, why not rate the taste and texture of mock meat by offering it to your dog? You can easily judge the quality by his level of interest. If he turns it down, it's not quite "meaty" enough, but if he devours it eagerly and quickly, it's sure to please even a finicky child's palate!

Here's another mock meat tip: freezing tofu gives it a meatier texture that's more satisfying to humans and canines alike. Freeze a package of tofu for two to three days. When ready to serve, thaw out the tofu by placing the package in a pot of gently simmering water for about 10 minutes. When thawed, transfer from package to a piece of unbleached cheesecloth, and squeeze out as much liquid as you can. It's now ready to replace sliced, diced, or shredded chicken in any recipe that calls for it.

really rewarDING rewards

When training a dog following the principles of positive reinforcement, it really helps to offer highly palatable treats as rewards for a job well done. Forget about those crunchy things packaged in boxes that pass as "dog treats"—those wouldn't motivate anyone to do anything. These soft, chewy, homemade tidbits, on the other hand, are excellent motivation for dogs to practice the obedience basics such as "Sit," "Stay," and "Down." Plus, they're easy enough to make that a child could do it by himself. And if you happen to get peckish while working on the training basics with your dog, it's fine to steal a few for yourself!

2 soy dogs
Ketchup

Preheat oven to 350°F. Cut soy dogs into bite-size pieces, about ½ inch thick, and arrange on a baking sheet. Spread each with a small amount of ketchup. Bake soy dog bits, ketchup side up, for 10 minutes. Let cool.

NOTE: If your dog prefers real-meat franks, by all means substitute beef or turkey hot dogs.

special OCCASIONS

Celebrations

COCKTAIL SOIRÉE

BIRTHDAY PARTY

FRRROZEN TRRREAT

· · · · · · · · ·

Dining Out (and In)

PICI'S KONG O'PLENTY

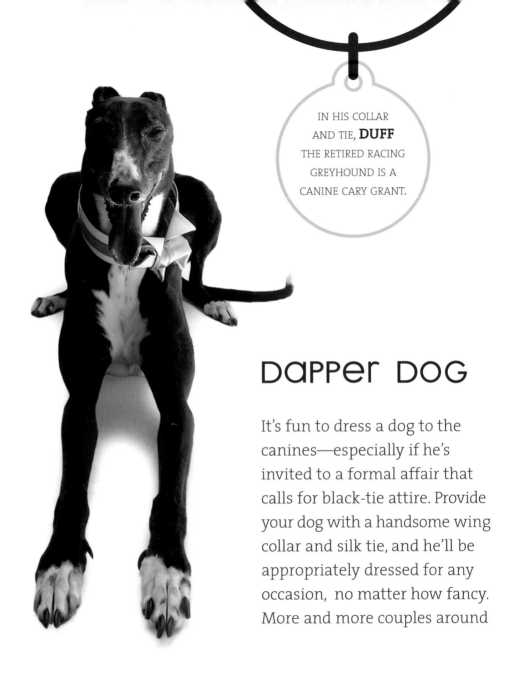

IN HIS COLLAR
AND TIE, **DUFF**
THE RETIRED RACING
GREYHOUND IS A
CANINE CARY GRANT.

Dapper Dog

It's fun to dress a dog to the canines—especially if he's invited to a formal affair that calls for black-tie attire. Provide your dog with a handsome wing collar and silk tie, and he'll be appropriately dressed for any occasion, no matter how fancy. More and more couples around

the world are including four-legged best friends in the wedding ceremony, adding a poignant, personal touch to the occasion. A simple haberdashery detail like this collar-and-tie ensemble will ensure that Fido's appearance is perfectly up to sniff when it's time to sit down to the reception feast!

After the big event, by all means provide your party-pooped pet with a soft place to rest his head, so he can digest the festive meal in comfort.

celebrations

When celebrating a special occasion, there is really no need to exclude the family dog. In fact, Fido's presence will make even the most festive occasion an affair to remember.

cocktail soirée

— ⦁ —

APPETIZERS

Olives
Cheese
Cheese Biscuits

DRINK

Hair of the Dog

appetizers

When having guests over for cocktails, cheese and olives are surefire crowd-pleasers. It's inevitable that Fido will score an hors d'oeuvre or two, but don't worry—olives are fine in moderation, and so is cheese (as long as it's not a super-rich, creamy Brie or Camembert, which could cause gastrointestinal upset). Go instead with something mild and firmer in texture, such as Gouda, Jarlsberg, Havarti, or Cheddar. As for the olives, might as well serve the best: Niçoise olives seasoned with herbes de Provence. (And if Fido should happen to ingest an olive pit, don't worry too much; it will most likely be eliminated the morning after.)

WHO ATE MY CHEESE?

Some dogs—and people—like their cheese served warm. Cheese biscuits are excellent as party hors d'oeuvres or as dog-training treats. They're so good that you may find your dog sitting in anticipation of a cheesy reward before you even utter the "sit" command! You may wish to make extra, as they do tend to disappear quickly; fortunately the recipe is simple and quick. If you like your biscuits spicy, go ahead and add 1 or 2 teaspoons crushed red pepper to the mixture in the food processor—but please remember to keep this batch separate from the one you share with your dog, so as not to cause him unnecessary stomach upset.

Don't try this at home; do cut cheese into bite-size portions.

CHeeseY
DOG-BONe BISCUITS

4 ounces extra-sharp Cheddar cheese, grated

4 tablespoons butter, softened and cut into 4 pieces

¾ cup all-purpose flour (plus more for rolling dough)

½ teaspoon salt

1 tablespoon half-and-half

Heat oven to 350°F. In a food processor, combine cheese, butter, flour, and salt, and pulse until mixture resembles coarse crumbs. Add half-and-half, and process on low speed until dough forms a ball.

On a lightly floured surface, using a lightly floured rolling pin, roll dough to a rectangle about 8 by 10 inches (it should be ⅛-inch thick). Cut biscuits with a dog bone-shaped cookie cutter, and transfer each "bone" to an ungreased cookie sheet, leaving a ¼-inch space between "bones." Bake 17 minutes, or until the edges are lightly browned. Let cool and serve.

HAIR OF THE DOG

Alcoholic beverages are a no-no for dogs. But there's one spirit that, if used properly, can be quite beneficial to Fido's health: Vodka. Here's how to emphasize the tail in cocktail: During tick season (which lasts from May through October), you may find one of these bloodsucking pests on your dog, putting him at risk for Lyme disease. But if you keep a bottle of vodka in the freezer, you have a most efficient tool for eliminating ticks. Simply pour a small shot of ice-cold vodka on the pest; the vodka combines with the frigid temperature to stun the tick, making it easy to pluck him from your beloved dog with a pair of tweezers. And if the brand you keep on hand is nothing less than the finest—Skyy— you can rest easy knowing that all your (human) cocktails will earn blue ribbons!

SKYY VODKA IS THE PREFERRED BRAND OF **SKY** THE WIRE-HAIRED FOX TERRIER. CHEERS!

Party Animals

Why kennel your dog while you're hosting a party for children? Invite Fido as the featured guest instead! Moms everywhere can relate: It can be tough coming up with an inventive children's-party theme that hasn't been done a million times. So why not get creative and make yours a pooch party? Celebrate the dog's birthday at the same time as your child's, and give the dog a matching party hat. Use brand-new dog bowls as festive tableware: Kids will have a blast eating human food from a doggie bowl. Or use tableware and mugs with a canine motif, such as the "Best Friend" Fiesta collection for Betty Crocker.

Safety is important on a special occasion like this. Remember that children love to share food with dogs, and a party atmosphere is all about cutting loose and having fun. Indulging in a little birthday cake once a year won't hurt your dog—as long as you're strict about having no chocolate anywhere on the menu. That way, if a child slips some birthday cake to the dog, or Fido picks up stray crumbs that will inevitably fall to the floor, it won't be a recipe for disaster ending with a trip to the emergency vet hospital.

GAMELY WEARING A "TICKLE ME ELMO" PARTY HAT, **CLEAVON** THE GREAT DANE IS THE LIFE OF THE PARTY.

carrot cupcakes

Children and dogs agree that carrot cake with cream cheese frosting is a delicious way to celebrate a birthday or any other special occasion; for safety, I've omitted nuts from the recipe, as nuts don't agree with all dogs (or kids). To be sure that everyone's portion is extra-moist and perfectly equal in size, make batches of carrot cupcakes instead of a single layer cake. The cupcakes are much easier for tiny fingers to handle—just unwrap and enjoy—and leftovers pack easily into tomorrow's lunch box for a day-after dessert.

for the batter:

¾ pound (about 2 ½ cups) finely grated carrots
2 cups all-purpose flour
1 teaspoon baking soda
1 ½ teaspoons baking powder

½ teaspoon ground cinnamon
4 large eggs
1 cup light brown sugar
1 cup safflower or canola oil
2 teaspoons pure vanilla extract

for the cream cheese frosting:

¼ cup unsalted butter, softened
   at room temperature
8 ounces cream cheese,
   softened at room temperature

1 ½ cups confectioner's sugar, sifted
1 teaspoon pure vanilla extract

Preheat oven to 350°F and place rack in center of oven. Place fluted liners in 18 muffin cups. Peel and grate carrots; set aside. In a separate bowl, whisk together the flour, baking soda, baking powder, and cinnamon; set aside.

In bowl of electric mixer, with the paddle attachment, beat the eggs until frothy (about one minute). Gradually add the sugar and beat until batter is thick and light in color (about 3 to 4 minutes). Add the oil in a steady stream, then the vanilla extract. Add the flour mixture and beat until just incorporated (don't over mix). With a large rubber spatula, gently fold in the grated carrots. Evenly divide the batter between the 18 muffin cups (fill each about two-thirds full) and bake 20 to 25 minutes or until a toothpick inserted in the center comes away clean. Combine frosting ingredients and top each cupcake with cream cheese frosting.

YIELD: 18 CUPCAKES

HARPO

THE CHIHUAHUA IS
THE SWEETEST
PETIT-FOUR ON
FOUR LEGS.

Frrrozen Trrreat

In general, dogs should not partake of dessert, as too much sugar is not good for them. However, canine gourmands do love the occasional lick of your ice-cream cone, which is safe so long as it's any flavor other than chocolate, with no chocolate chips or swirls. So why not make a special-occasion cold dessert dogs can share? Simply open a can of unsweetened pumpkin puree (dogs adore it), spoon out three or four tablespoons, and top with a half-scoop of rich, creamy vanilla ice cream or gelato. For human portions, reverse the equation by starting with two generous scoops of vanilla ice cream or gelato, then topping with two tablespoons pumpkin puree. Finish by dusting lightly with cinnamon.

Pumpkin puree + vanilla gelato = virtuous treat (well, almost)

canine culinary caveat

Dogs should never eat chocolate, as the theobromine in the cocoa causes a toxic reaction. Dark or unsweetened baking chocolate is especially toxic, as it contains higher levels of theobromine, so be especially careful to close your dog out of the kitchen when cooking or baking with chocolate. (If you suspect that your dog may have ingested chocolate, rush him to the emergency veterinary hospital without delay.)

The only way that dogs and chocolate can safely mix is in one of the delightfully realistic canine molds created by the brilliant Belgian chocolatier Martine's Chocolates. This chocolate Collie is so realistic, in fact, he's a ringer for the world-famous Lassie!

This splendid crystal dog bowl by Sheila
Parness bears the apt Latin legend,
Fidelis Atque Constans

DINING OUT

Any time the weather permits is a great time to take a break from cooking at home, put on nice clothes, and dine out alfresco. While you're enjoying a respite from your hot kitchen, why not bring Fido along? All he needs is a dish of water, something most restaurants are happy to provide. Here, Johan and Tama anticipate a wonderful meal at chef John Villa's Dominic Restaurant in downtown Manhattan; with the couple is their majestic Leonberger, Milo.

Remember that sidewalks heat up like griddles during a hot day, and they retain heat well into the evening hours (even after dark). While dogs do love to be included in everything we do and eat, remember that canine safety is always the priority. Hot pavement is not a safe place for a dog to recline—especially if the dog is a cold-weather breed such as the Saint Bernard; any giant breed, such as the Leonberger, Newfoundland, or Great Dane; or a short-muzzled (bracycephalic) breed, such as the Pug, Pekingese, or any variety of bulldog. These dogs don't do well in hot weather, and are especially vulnerable to heat stroke. So if the temperature is in the 80 to 90°F range (or higher), please leave your dog at home to bask in the air-conditioned interior. He'll appreciate your thoughtfulness!

This special greaseproof bag is provided with the compliments of your host.

Doggie Bag

Oh where, oh where have
your leftovers gone?

Oh where, oh where
can they be?

If you've had all
you can possibly eat,

Please bring the rest
home to me!!

Of course, if the food you're dining out on is suitable for Fido—i.e., it contains no harmful ingredients such as chocolate or onions—and you can't quite finish your entree, by all means bring home some leftovers. That's what "doggie bags" are for. This one has an illustrious history: first created in 1949 by the Chicago company Bagcraft, it's still used at restaurants all over the United States.

DINING IN

A stay-at-home dog doesn't have to miss out on serious fun while you dine out in hot weather. Leave him in air-conditioned comfort with Pici's Kong o'Plenty. The main ingredient of this special, homemade pup-sicle treat is the Kong, an industrial-strength rubber toy that's one of the most brilliant dog playthings ever invented. Named for my champion chewer Pici, the Kong o'Plenty is designed to keep your dog happily occupied for the duration of your meal, as he works hard to reach the delicacies buried inside it.

PICI'S
KONG O'PLENTY

1 small piece of bread
1 rubber Kong chew toy
4 tablespoons beef or
   chicken stock

4 tablespoons all-natural peanut
   butter (with no additives,
   preferably organic) or 2
   wedges Gruyère cheese,
   softened at room temperature
1 leaf of lettuce, for garnish

Plug the small hole at the tip of the Kong toy with some bread. Pour in the stock to cover about an inch of the Kong, and freeze until stock is frozen. When ready to serve, remove from freezer. Using a spoon, spread the top half of the interior walls of the Kong with the peanut butter or cheese; garnish with the lettuce and serve.

STYLISH DINING
accessories

—— ✖ ——

Tableware is much more than an accessory; it's the first step to a healthy dog meal. Cheap plastic bowls are a no-no. Only high-quality plastic dishes—the food-grade kind used for humans—should be used for dogs, as cheap plastic harbors bacteria and imparts a taste to water and food that some dogs can't stand. They might actually refuse to drink if the only available water comes in a cheap plastic bowl, and such abstinence can lead to serious health problems. Metal and ceramic bowls are the safest bet for serving food and water to dogs. Of course, if you prefer to go over the top with posh canine tableware that coordinates with your own, there are many chic options, including collectible Fiesta bowls emblazoned with the legend GOOD DOG.

BLUE PLATE SPECIAL

As for what you choose to set your table with, why not opt for plates tough enough to stand up to anything your dog can dish out? In our animal house, before rolling up our sleeves to tackle the dishes, we like to "pre-wash" by putting plates on the floor so the dogs may lick them clean.

Of course, in their diligent zeal to remove every last morsel, the dogs won't hesitate to stand on the plates. That's why we only eat from durable, elegant, vitrified china by Homer Laughlin, makers of Fiesta. Homer Laughlin's foodservice collection is the choice of restaurants and hotels nationwide. And with good

This ultra-chic bowl (left) is an ingenious product of the Italian firm Alessi.

reason: So far, these tough-as-nails plates have survived accidentally falling to the floor from table height, and not a single one has been damaged by my hungry dogs, who range in size from 45 to 80 pounds. That's a lot of dog standing on a little plate. Call it the *Bow Wow Chow* seal of approval!

resource guide

—⋈—

TITLE PAGE: "Bow Wow Chow" plate available at Sylvester & Co., Sag Harbor, NY, 631-725-5012

PAGE 8: Red takeout container from Doggone Good!, 800-660-2665 or *www.doggonegood.com*

PAGE 10: Heart-shaped "Mimi's Bowl" (top) from Cats Rule/Dogs 2, available at Petco stores, *www.petco.com*; for more stores, visit *www.catsrule.com*. Aqua dog bowl by Bauer Pottery (also available in red) from Frank J. Miele Gallery, NYC, 212-249-7250

PAGE 11: For information on Purina HA, available by prescription, ask your veterinarian or visit *www.purina.com*

PAGE 17: Fiesta "Good Dog" bowl in Shamrock from Sylvester & Co., Sag Harbor, NY, 631-725-5012

PAGE 19: Heart-shaped pot by LeCreuset available at Bloomingdale's, *www.bloomingdales.com*; for more stores, call 1-800-CREUSET or visit *www.lecreuset.com*

PAGE 20: Vintage dog bowls by Robinson Ransbottom Pottery (pictured) are highly collectible, and occasionally available on eBay, *www.ebay.com;* Animal Allergy and Dermatology Specialists, NYC, 212-206-0969 or *www.animalallergyandderm.com*

PAGE 21: Tam-o-shanter by Robert Mackie of Scotland, Holm Mill, Stewarton, available at Scottish Products, NYC, 646-742-0908

PAGE 23: For stores carrying fruit and vegetable wash by Healthy Harvest, call 203-245-2033

PAGE 24: For stores carrying Arrowhead Mills buckwheat pancake mix, call 800-434-4246 or visit *www.arrowheadmills.com*

A WARNING ABOUT NON-STICK COOKWARE: If you have pet birds, do not use any non-stick cookware, cooking tool, or appliance—the resultant fumes can cause fatal respiratory damage.

PAGE 28: Whole-wheat bagels courtesy of Hot & Crusty Bagel Cafe, NYC, 212-753-2614

PAGE 29: To learn more about the self-discipline of Gallic females, read *French Women Don't Get Fat: The Secret of Eating for Pleasure* by Mireille Guiliano (Knopf), available at *www.amazon.com*

PAGE 31: "Ryan's Bowl" by Cats Rule/Dogs2 available at Petco stores, *www.petco.com*, and Fauna Foods, *www.faunafoods.com* (or visit *www.catsrule.com*)

PAGE 32: For information on the Brita water filtration system, call 800-24-Brita or visit *www.Brita.com*; "Thirsty" bowl by Wagwear from Fetch, *www.fetchpets.com*

PAGE 37: In our animal house, the favorite noodle is any shape by Bionaturae, makers of organic pasta; for stores, call 860-642-6996 or visit *www.bionaturae.com*. White Fiesta "Good Dog" bowl from Sylvester & Co., 631-725-5012

PAGE 44: Silver leather dog collar with red leather flower ornament by Poochee, to order from Trixie & Peanut, *www.trixieandpeanut.com*

PAGE 45: Oil mister by Bodum available at *www.bodum.com*

PAGE 47: Foreman Double Knockout Grill from Macy's, www.macys.com; for more stores, visit *www.esalton.com*

PAGE 51: Szeged paprika (hot or sweet) available at Otto's Hungarian Import Store and Deli, 818-845-0433 or *www.hungariandeli.com*; for information on the Pick Szalami and Szeged Paprika Museum in Hungary (!), visit *www.museum.hu/szeged/pick*

PAGE 54: Bespoke polka-dotted chef's toque and bib to order from Paw & Chic, 866-995-9161, *www.pawandchic.com*; 12-quart stockpot by LeCreuset from Bloomingdale's, *www.bloomingdales.com* (for more stores, call 800-CREUSET or visit *www.lecreuset.com*)

PAGE 56: Dogs like eating soup from a bowl with a rubber ring to prevent sliding. Blue metal rubber-ringed dog bowl (also available in orange, red, yellow, and two shades of green) by Prima Pet from Fetch, *www.fetchpets.com*, or Doggone Good!, *www.doggonegood.com*

PAGE 61: Breath-a-licious dental bone from Dancing Paws, 888-644-8297 or *www.dancingpaws.com*; "Material Dog" Crypton Super Fabric designed by William Wegman, 800-CRYPTON or *www.cryptonfabric.com*

PAGE 66: Earthenware popcorn bowl from Crate & Barrel, 800-967-6696 or *www.crateandbarrel.com*

PAGE 67: Dinner Party seasoning by Halo, Purely for Pets available at Pet Stop, 212-580-2400 or *www.petstopnyc.com* (for more stores, call 800-426-4256 or visit *www.halopets.com*). Nothing tastes better than popcorn popped on the stovetop in a Whirley-Pop popper, available at Broadway Panhandler, *www.broadwaypanhandler.com* (for more stores, call 219-984-9996 or visit *www.wabashvalleyfarms.com*). For a delicious shortcut, I use Garden of Eatin' organic microwave popcorn; for stores, call 800-434-4246 or visit *www.gardenofeatin.com*

PAGE **71:** Organic raw beef bone from K.E. Rush & Sons, 215-412-4110 or *www.natures-intent.com*

PAGE **74:** Chickettes is a registered trademark of Worthington Foods, *www.worthingtonfoods.com;* Smart Dogs and Tofu Pups are registered trademarks of Light Life Foods, 800-SOY-EASY or *www.lightlife.com*

PAGE **78:** Man's wing collar, stud, and gray silk tie from A.T. Harris Formalwear, NYC, 212-682-6325

PAGE **81:** Niçoise olives and porcelain olive tray from Fig & Olive Kitchen & Tasting Bar, NYC, 212-207-4555

PAGE **83:** Dog-bone-shaped cookie cutters (in several sizes) from New York Cake Supplies, 800-942-2539, *www.nycake.com*

PAGE **84:** To learn more about Skyy Vodka, visit *www.skyy.com*

PAGE **86:** For information on Betty Crocker "Best Friend" special-edition Fiesta, call 800-432-4959 or visit *www.bettycrocker.com*

PAGE **90:** Paper doily from New York Cake Supplies, 800-942-2539, *www.nycake.com*

PAGE 91: Vanilla gelato from Il Laboratorio del Gelato, NYC, 212-343-9922 or *www.laboratoriodelgelato.com*

PAGE 92: Chocolate dog from Martine's Chocolates, 212-744-6289 or *www.martineschocolates.com*

PAGE 93: crystal dog bowl by Sheila Parness; to order, email *sheila.parness@parness.com*

Help your dog dine in comfort by raising his bowls up off the floor. Bent plywood feeders by Holden Designs Inc. from Postmodern Pets, 650-331-3500 or www.postmodernpets.com

PAGE 94: Dominic Restaurant, NYC, 212-343-0700, *www.dominicrestaurant.com*

PAGE 96: To order the original "Doggie Bag" by Bagcraft, call 800-621-8468 or visit *www.bagcraft.com*

PAGE 99: Kong products available at Petco stores, *www.petco.com*; for more stores, call 303-216-2626 or visit *www.kongcompany.com*

PAGE 101: Fiesta "Good Dog" bowl in sunflower from Sylvester & Co, 631-725-5012

PAGE 102: Alessi Lupita dog bowl from Postmodern Pets, 650-331-3500 or *www.postmodernpets.com*

acknowledgments

—————— ✖ ——————

THE AUTHOR EXTENDS HEARTFELT THANKS TO THE FOLLOWING, WITHOUT WHOM THIS BOOK WOULD NOT HAVE BEEN POSSIBLE:

Project manager Sandra Gilbert, Zaro Weil, Ljiljana Baird, Sarah Rainwater, Tomoko Shimura, George and Martha Szabo, Leica Camera, Todd Oldham, Gary Kaskel and United Action for Animals, Susan Richmond and everyone at The Humane Society of New York, Dr. Heather Peikes, Christine Butler, Kerry, Mary Ann, Jerry, and John Villa, Shannon Reed, Ani Antreasyan, Sue Grundfest, and Robin Bell, with special thanks to John Maher.

TREATS ARE IN ORDER FOR OUR YOUNG HUMAN MODELS, KYLE ERF AND DEA BROGAARD THOMPSON, AND FOR ALL THE DOGS WHO POSED FOR THE PHOTOGRAPHS, THEY ARE (IN ORDER OF APPEARANCE):

Daoosa, Pepper, Sheba, Ellie, Coco, Naco, Luca, Kipling, Sam, Billie, Boomer, Milo the mutt, Duff, Olive, Sky, Cleavon, Harpo, Milo the Leonberger, Thumper.

Published by MQ Publications Limited
12 The Ivories, 6-8 Northampton Street
London N1 2HY
Tel: +44 (0) 20 7359 2244, fax: +44 (0) 20 7359 1616
e-mail: mail@mqpuablications.com
www.mqpublications.com

Author photo by Todd Oldham

Editor: Sandra Gilbert
Designer: Sarah Rainwater

ISBN: 1-84072-977-5
10 9 8 7 6 5 4 3 2 1

Printed and bound in Italy.

No small part of the pleasure of having a pet is the uniqueness of each animal.
Because dogs vary widely in terms of physical characteristics and care needs, it
is important to consult with your pet's veterinarian before implementing any
dietary change described in this book. The information contained in this book
is based upon sources that the author believes to be reliable. Information
relating to products and companies is current as of June 1, 2005.